McDonnell Douglas
F-4 Phantom II
at George Air Force Base, California
1964-1992

Schiffer Publishing Ltd

4880 Lower Valley Road • Atglen, PA 19310

ACKNOWLEDGMENTS

I would like to thank the following photographers without whose images I could not have put this book together: Mike Anselmo, Tom Brewer, David F. Brown, Jim Goodall, Robert Greby, Phil Huston, Craig Kaston, Ben Knowles, Ray Leader, Bob Leavitt, James P. Loomis, Frank MacSorley, Bill Malerba, Don McGarry, Paul Minert, Rick Morgan, Jack D. Morris, Kevin Patrick, Doug Remington, Brian C. Rogers, Mick Roth, Jim Rotramel, Bob Shane, Keith Snyder, Keith Svendsen, Norman E. Taylor, Jim Tunney, Scott Van Aken, Peter Wilson, Scott R. Wilson, and Jim Wooley.

I also want to thank William R. Peake and Brian C. Rogers who have helped with the historical information, and have proofread and fact-checked the manuscript.

Copyright © 2018 by Don Logan

Library of Congress Control Number: 2017949940

"Schiffer," "Schiffer Publishing, Ltd.," and the pen and inkwell logo are registered trademarks of Schiffer Publishing, Ltd.

Type set in Eurostile

ISBN: 978-0-7643-5449-6

Printed in China

Published by Schiffer Publishing, Ltd.
4880 Lower Valley Road
Atglen, PA 19310
Phone: (610) 593-1777;
Fax: (610) 593-2002
E-mail: Info@schifferbooks.com
www.schifferbooks.com

For our complete selection of fine books on this and related subjects, please visit our website at www.schifferbooks.com. You may also write for a free catalog.

Schiffer Publishing's titles are available at special discounts for bulk purchases for sales promotions or premiums. Special editions, including personalized covers, corporate imprints, and excerpts, can be created in large quantities for special needs. For more information, contact the publisher.

We are always looking for people to write books on new and related subjects. If you have an idea for a book, please contact us at proposals@schifferbooks.com.

CONTENTS

INTRODUCTION

With the arrival of the first McDonnell-Douglas F-4s and F-4Cs on April 6, 1964, the association of George Air Force Base, California and the F-4 began. This association would last over twenty-eight years. The initial mission was to train F-4 aircrews. From 1964 through 1973, the majority of the graduates went directly to South East Asia in support of the Vietnam War. As the need for newly trained aircrews decreased, the 35th Tactical Fighter Wing (TFW), and later the 37th TFW, added an operational commitment flying F-4Es along with the F-4C Wild Weasel and F-4G Advanced Wild Weasel aircraft. The training of aircrews for the German Air Force was added to the 35th TFW's mission in December 1972. F-4 Operations continued at George under the 35th and 37th Wings until inactivation of the 35th Wing in December 1992.

69-7561, an F-4G-44 MC, and 66-0303, an F-4E-32 MC, both belonging to the 561st TFS, 37th TFW fly in formation over the southern end of the Sierra Nevada mountains. The F-4G is armed with an AGM-78 Standard Anti-Radiation missile and an AGM-45 Shrike Anti-Radiation missile. The F-4E is carrying an AGM-45 Shrike Anti-Radiation missile. Both are carrying an AN/ALQ-119 ECM Pod. *USAF Photo*

GEORGE AIR FORCE BASE

George Air Force Base (AFB) is a former United States Air Force (USAF) base located within city limits, eight miles northwest of central Victorville, California, about seventy-five miles northeast of Los Angeles, California. The facility was closed by the Base Realignment and Closure (BRAC) 1992 commission at the end of the Cold War. It is now the site of the Southern California Logistics Airport.

George AFB was named in honor of Brig. Gen. Harold Huston George, who was a World War I fighter ace, serving with both the 185th and 139th Aero Squadrons. At the beginning of World War II, he was assigned to V Interceptor Command, Far East Air Force in the Philippines.

Established by the United States Army Air Corps as an Advanced Flying School in June 1941, George was closed at the end of World War II. It was again activated as a training base by the USAF in November 1950, five months after the outbreak of the Korean War. It remained a training base throughout the Cold War, primarily for training Tactical Air Command pilots in frontline USAF fighters until its closing in 1993.

George AFB was officially decommissioned in December 1992. In 1993, President Bill Clinton announced a "Five Part Plan" to speed economic recovery in communities where military bases were to be closed. One part of this plan called for improving public participation in the base's environmental cleanup program. George AFB was among a number of installations where environmental cleanup was placed on a "fast track" so base property could be quickly transferred to the community for reuse. Many of the old base housing and buildings are currently used by the Army and Marine Corps for urban warfare training.

The three-prison Federal Correctional Complex, Victorville, is located on some of the base's former lands.

Since 2009, the California Air National Guard's 196th Reconnaissance Squadron (96th RS) has operated an MQ-1 Predator Remotely Piloted Aircraft (RPA) training facility at the Southern California Logistics Airport.

32nd/8th Tactical Fighter Wing

On April 1, 1964, the 32nd Tactical Fighter Wing (TFW) was activated and organized at George. Three fighter squadrons (68th, 433rd, and 497th) were equipped with F-4Ds. On June 18, 1964, the 8th Tactical Fighter Wing was reassigned without personnel or equipment to George AFB from Itazuke AB, Japan as part of an overall effort to reduce the number of wings in Japan. The 8th TFW replaced and absorbed the resources of the 32nd TFW.

While at George AFB, the wing trained with the McDonnell-Douglas F-4D Phantom II fighter aircraft. The 68th Tactical Fighter Squadron (TFS) deployed to Korat Royal Thai Air Force Base (RTAFB) Thailand during July–December 1964, with the wing participating in numerous exercises, operational readiness inspections, and the like.

The entire 8th TFW was reassigned to Ubon Royal Thai Air Force Base, Thailand in December 1965, to commence combat operations in the Vietnam War.

479th Tactical Fighter Wing

The 479th Fighter-Bomber Wing was activated at George AFB on December 1, 1952.

The 479th, then a Tactical Fighter Wing, gained four McDonnell-Douglas F-4C Phantom II Combat Crew Training Squadrons in December 1965 (68th TFS, 71st TFS, 431st TFS, plus one other, for four squadrons total), and began F-4D replacement training in February 1967.

The 479th began training foreign personnel in F-4 operations and maintenance in March 1969, including pilots from Israel, Iran, Japan, and West Germany. The 479th was inactivated and replaced by the 35th TFW in October 1971.

35th Tactical Fighter Wing/Tactical Training Wing

The 35th Tactical Fighter Wing reactivated at George Air Force Base, California, on October 1, 1971, where it replaced the 479th Tactical Fighter Wing. The wing's mission at George was to take over the mission of training F-4 flight crews.

With the arrival of F-105F/G aircraft from the 388th TFW at Korat Royal Thai Air Force Base (RTAFB), Thailand in July 1973, the wing began training aircrews for radar detection and suppression or "Wild Weasel" missions in addition to other F-4 training. By 1975, with the arrival of new F-4G aircraft, the wing was training aircrews exclusively in Wild Weasel.

Operations at George Air Force Base were reorganized by mission requirements March 30, 1981. The 35th Tactical Fighter Wing retained control of the 20th and 21st Tactical Fighter Training Squadrons, and gained the 39th Tactical Fighter Squadron.

With the inactivation of the 39th Tactical Fighter Squadron in 1985, the 35th Tactical Fighter Wing was redesignated the 35th Tactical Training Wing.

37th Tactical Fighter Wing

The new 37th Tactical Fighter Wing assumed the 561st Tactical Fighter Squadron (TFS), 562nd Tactical Fighter Training Squadron (TFTS), and 563rd Tactical Fighter Squadron (TFS) for active Wild Weasel missions in 1981. This training ended in 1989 when the 37th TFW was reassigned to the Tonopah Test Range in Nevada, assuming F-117A operational development.

Operations at George Air Force Base were reorganized again October 5, 1989. The 37th Tactical Fighter Wing and the 35th Tactical Training Wing consolidated all operations under the newly redesignated 35th Tactical Fighter Wing. Under the reorganization the 35th regained control of the 561st Tactical Fighter Squadron and the 562nd Tactical Fighter Training Squadron.

Caption Notes

Identification of the aircraft in the caption is in the following format:

F-4W-XX MC YY-ZZZ, where W is the aircraft type "C," "D," "E," "F," or "G."

XX is the manufacturers Block Number

MC is the manufacturer's ID – McDonnell Douglas, St. Louis,

YY is a two-digit number indicating the contract year group

ZZZZ is the individual serial number within the year group.

Unit, Date, Location etc. in the captions come directly from information written on the color slide mount by the photographer.

8TH TACTICAL FIGHTER WING

The 32nd TFW was activated at George AFB on April 6, 1964, to begin training in the F-4C. On June 18, 1964, the wing moved from Itazuke AB, Japan, without personnel or equipment to George AFB, California, absorbing resources of the 32nd TFW. The 32nd TFW was inactivated on July 25, 1964. For the next year, the 8th TFW trained with F-4 aircraft. While at George AFB the 68th TFS, 431st TFS, 433rd TFS, and 497th TFS were assigned to the 8th TFW. The 8th TFW F-4s did not have tail codes while at George. It moved to Ubon RTAFB, Thailand, on December 6, 1965, and commenced combat operations, including bombardment, ground support, air defense, interdiction, and armed reconnaissance.

479TH TACTICAL FIGHTER WING

The Wing was established as the 479th Fighter Group on October 12, 1943. The unit trained for combat in P-38 and P-40 aircraft and served as an air defense organization from October 1943 through April 1944. It moved to England in May 1944, joining the 8th Air Force. The 479th flew combat in Europe from May 26, 1944 until April 25, 1945, escorting heavy bombers during operations against targets on the continent, strafing targets of opportunity, and flying fighter-bomber, counter air, and area patrol sorties. During the D-Day invasion on June 6, 1944, aircraft of the 479th patrolled the beachhead from dawn until well after dark. They participated in the Battle of the Bulge (December 1944 through January 1945) by escorting bombers and strafing transportation targets while on escort duty.

The 479th replaced the 131st Fighter-Bomber Wing at George AFB in December 1952, where it remained until its inactivation on October 1, 1971. From January 1953, they trained as a fighter-bomber, and later, as a fighter-day group, employing F-51 and F-86 aircraft. It converted to F-100s beginning in September 1954, and to F-104s beginning in October 1958. The 479th deployed one F-104 squadron at the Naval Air Station (NAS) Key West, Florida, during the Cuban Missile Crisis in October 1962. During 1965, the 479th deployed three F-104 squadrons to Taiwan and South Vietnam to provide air defenses in the northern area of South Vietnam. Again, in mid-1966, it transferred one F-104 squadron to Southeast Asia. The 479th continued F-104 replacement training until transferring all of its F-104s to Luke AFB, Arizona, in July 1967.

The 479th TFW gained two F-4C squadrons (68th TFS and 431st TFS) from the 8th TFW on December 6, 1965, and the 4452nd CCTS activated on January 16, 1968. F-4 replacement training started in February of 1966. The 479th TFS was assigned to the 479th TFW on July 29, 1966, followed by the 434th TFS on November 1, 1966.

On the initial assignment of tail codes, the 68th TFS, 431st TFS, 434th TFS, 476th TFS, and 4452nd Combat Crew Training Squadron (CCTS) were assigned GA, GB, GC, GD, and GE tail codes, respectively. However, the GA tail code was not used by the 68th TFS as the squadron was reassigned before the codes could be applied, so the 4535th CCTS (activated in October 1968) used GA instead. The 476th TFS did not carry the assigned GD tail code, as the squadron was inactivated on September 25, 1968. The GD tall code was assumed by the 434th TFS after the GC tail code had been used for a short period. The 4452nd CCTS applied the GC code to their F-4s.

The 4546th TFRS/TFTS/TTS was also assigned to the 479th TFW, flying F-4s with a red and white checkered fin cap and the GB tail code. The 4546th TTS is not listed by official sources, but was assigned between 1970 and 1971. The 4546th was the squadron that trained the author as an F-4 crewmember.

On October 1, 1971, the 35th TFW replaced the 479th TFW, at George AFB, and all remaining coded units were reassigned to the 35th TFW. The 479th TFW inactivated until assigned to Holloman AFB in 1978, activated as the unit flying AT-38s as part of the Fighter Lead In Training program.

479th TFW –
1965 until October 1, 1971

GA	68th TFS	December 6, 1965 to 4535th CCTS
GB	431st TFS	Early 1965 to 4546th TFTS/TFRS
GC	434th TFS	December 6, 1965 to 4452nd CCTS
GD	476th TFS	Early 1965 to 434th TFS
GE	4452nd CCTS	January 16, 1968

68th TFS

F-4D-27 MC 65-0644 of the 68th TFS, photographed on March 30, 1968, at Andrews AFB. *Photo by Jack D. Morris*

F-4D-29 MC 65-0797 of the 68th TFS, photographed on March 30, 1968, at Andrews AFB. *Photo by Jack D. Morris*

4535th CCTS

F-4C-19 MC 63-7529 of the 4535th CCTS/479th TFW, photographed in September 1970. *Don Logan Collection*

F-4C-24 MC 64-0841 of the 4535th CCTS/479th TFW, photographed on November 18, 1970. *Tom Brewer Collection*

F-4D-28 MC 65-0747 of 4535th CCTS/479th TFW, at Andrews AFB, on May 18, 1969. *Photo by Frank MacSorley*

F-4E-38 MC 68-0391 of the 4535th CCTS/479th TFW. *Don Logan Collection*

431st TFS/4546th TFTS/TFRS/TTS

F-4D-29 MC 66-7466 of the 431st TFS/479th TFW, at Van Nuys ANGB, in July 1968. *Don Logan Collection*

F-4E-37 MC 68-0310 of the 431st TFS/479th TFW, photographed in September 1969, at Eglin AFB. *Photo by Jack D. Morris*

F-4C-19 MC 63-7530 of the 4546th TFRS/479th TFW performs a close pass for a safety check to ensure the dart tow target and its tow cable were successfully jettisoned, in June 1971. *Photo by Don Logan*

F-4C-19 MC 63-7530 of the 4546th TFRS/479th TFW, carrying a dart tow target, sits in the arming area at the end of the runway awaiting takeoff, in June 1971. *Photo by Don Logan*

F-4C-21 MC 63-7667 of the 4546th TFRS/479th TFW, at Eglin AFB, on May 30, 1971. *Tom Brewer Collection*

F-4C-18 MC 63-7506 of the 4546th TFRS/479th TFW, in June 1971, the aircraft is carrying a SUU-23 M-61 gun pod on the centerline pylon and a SUU-20 practice bomb dispenser on the two inboard pylons. *Photo by Don Logan*

F-4C-18 MC 63-7507 of the 4546th TFRS/479th TFW, at Andrews AFB. *Tom Brewer Collection*

This image was photographed from the back seat of number four in a F-4C four ship formation. The other three F-4Cs are seen in echelon formation. The three 4546th TFRS F-4Cs are -20 MC 63-7649, -22 MC 64-0679, and -18 MC 63-7511. *Photo by Don Logan*

Two views of formation takeoffs of a 4546th TFRS F-4C, from the rear cockpit of the wingman, in July 1971. *Photo by Don Logan*

F-4E-36 MC 67-0371 of the 4546th TFRS/479th TFW, at Eglin AFB. *Tom Brewer Collection*

F-4E-37 MC 67-0362 of the 4546th TFRS/479th TFW, at George AFB. *Tom Brewer Collection*

4452nd CCTS

F-4C-19 MC 63-7569 of the 4452nd CCTS/479th TFW, at George AFB. *Tom Brewer Collection*

F-4C-21 MC 63-7666 of the 4452nd CCTS/479th TFW, in July 1970, at George AFB. *Don Logan Collection*

F-4E-38 MC 68-0362 of the 4452nd CCTS/479th TFW. *Photo by Jim Rotramel*

F-4E-37 MC 67-0356 of the 4452nd CCTS/479TFW, at Eglin AFB. *Tom Brewer Collection*

434th TFS

F-4E-40 MC 68-0479 of the 434th TFS/479th TFW with a multi-colored flagship tail stripe. *Don Logan Collection*

F-4E-40 MC 68-0479 of the 434th TFS/479th TFW with another version of the multi-colored flagship tail stripe. *Don Logan Collection*

F-4E-37 MC 66-0347 of the 434th TFS/479th TFW in Thunderbirds practice markings, at Andrews AFB, on May 10, 1969.
Photo by Jack D. Morris

F-4E-37 MC 66-0347 of the 434th TFS/479th TFW, at Wright-Patterson AFB, on October 30, 1971. *Photo by Jack D. Morris*

F-4E-38 MC 68-0395 of the 434th TFS/479th TFW, at George AFB, in September 1970. *Don Logan Collection*

F-4E-41 MC 68-0505 of the 434th TFS/479th TFW, at George AFB November 18, 1970. *Tom Brewer Collection*

831ST AIR DIVISION

The 831st Air Division was activated at George in 1980, replacing Tactical Training, George, which had been the headquarters for George's training operations. A few months after the division's activation, F-4 training operations were split, with one wing (35th TFW) using F-4Es to train United States and foreign fighter aircrews, and the other wing (37th TFS) flying F-4Gs to train Wild Weasel crews. In 1989, it was announced that George would be closing. Training operations were consolidated into a single wing (35th TTW), and the division was inactivated in 1991, as operations at George were reduced.

F-4E-60 MC 74-1045, marked as the 12 Air Force flagship 562nd TFS, photographed on April 20, 1990. *Photo by Phil Huston*

831st AIR DIVISION

F-4E-36 MC 67-0389, marked as the 831st AD of the 431st TFTS, on June 13, 1970, at Perrin AFB, Texas. *Photo by Norman E. Taylor*

F-4E-34 MC 67-0249, marked as the 831st AD with 35th TFW, and 37th TFW emblems on the intake, in April 1997. *Photo by Bob Shane*

F-4E-34 MC 67-0249, marked as the 831st of the 35th TFW, photographed on June 6, 1987. *Photo by Bob Leavitt*

F-4E-51 MC 72-0141, marked as the 831st AD of the 35th FW, on December 1, 1990. *Photo by Norman E. Taylor*

35TH TACTICAL FIGHTER WING/35TH TACTICAL TRAINING WING

The 35th was established as 35th Fighter Wing on August 10, 1948. Activated on August 18, 1948, it flew air defense missions in Japan from August 1948 through November 1950. In July 1950, the wing's tactical group and two squadrons deployed to Korea for combat, but the wing (with one assigned and one attached squadron) continued flying air defense missions in Japan as well as photographic reconnaissance of the Japanese coasts. Wing headquarters moved without personnel or equipment to South Korea on December 1, 1950, assuming resources of the 6150th Tactical Support Wing. F-51 aircraft were used in combat operations, including armed reconnaissance, bomber escort, interdiction, and ground support.

Organized again in April 1966, at Da Nang AB, South Vietnam, replacing the 6252nd Tactical Fighter Wing, the 35th controlled two F-4C squadrons, two rotational B-57 squadrons, and F-102 flights of the 64th Fighter-Interceptor Squadron. On October 1, 1966, the 35th and 366th Wings moved in name only; the 35th Wing replacing the 366th Wing at Phan Rang AB, South Vietnam, and becoming an F-100 organization. The two B-57 squadrons also shifted bases, following the 35th Wing to Phan Rang. The 35th gained an A-37B squadron (8th Special Operations Squadron) in September 1970.

It began phasing down for inactivation in April 1971, standing down from operations on June 26, 1971. Remaining resources passed to the 315th Tactical Airlift Wing on July 31, 1971, when the 35th Wing inactivated. A few months later, on October 1, 1971, the 35th Wing activated at George AFB, California, replacing the 479th Tactical Fighter Wing. The 35th TFW provided F-4 aircrew and maintenance personnel replacement training. It also participated in tactical exercises, tests, and operations. F-105 Wild Weasel units became part of the wing in July 1973. The 35th began Wild Weasel (radar detection and suppression) aircrew training in F-105 and F-4 aircraft in late 1975. It lost Wild Weasel assets in March 1981 to the 37th TFW, a second tactical wing that activated at George AFB. The 35th was redesignated a Tactical Training Wing (TTW) on July 1, 1984, but retained an air defense augmentation responsibility. In addition, from 1981 to 1991, wing personnel advised specific Air National Guard units on F-4 operations. The wing's structure allowed for a dual-role mission, combat and training. The 35th TTW regained the Wild Weasel training mission in September 1989, when the 37th TFW moved to Tonopah, Nevada, to become the first F-117 wing.

As part of the 35th TTW's 20th TFTS, the German Luftwaffe undertook its F-4 training at George AFB. This started with the F-4F in standard Luftwaffe camouflage with USAF markings and codes, and later with specially purchased 1975 block F-4Es in full USAF camouflage and markings, all under the designation of the 1st German Air Force Training Squadron (GAFTS).

From August 1990 until March 1991, the 561st Squadron with F-4Gs deployed to the island state of Bahrain for both training and combat operations in southwest Asia. The 561st also rotated troops and aircraft to the Persian Gulf as part of the on-going US presence in southwest Asia, beginning in June 1991, and following with ninety-day deployments. The 35th began phasing down for inactivation and base closure in mid-1991. The wing's flying squadrons departed or inactivated by July 1992, and the wing remained non-operational until inactivated in December 1992. It replaced Air Forces Iceland at Keflavik NAS in May 1993.

The 35th Tactical Fighter Wing activation at George AFB took place prior to the common wing tail code, at that time each squadron had its own individual code: initial units were the 4535th CCTS (GB), the 4452nd CCTS (GC), the 434th TFS (GD), and the 35th OMS (GE) with the Bombing Range Support UH-1. The 35th TFW became the major F-4 training wing, and under the common wing tail code concept, all the wing squadrons recoded to GA. The 4535th CCTS and 4452nd CCTS inactivated on December 1, 1972, and were replaced by the 20th TFTS and 21st TFTS.

The Wild Weasel role was first assigned to the 35th TFW with the F-105. The 561st TFS, 562nd TFS, and the 563rd TFTS were added in 1973, 1974, and 1975, respectively, and the three eventually transitioned to the F-4G as the conversion production line permitted, starting on April 28, 1978. The Weasel squadrons also operated the F-4E, and by June 1979, the 35th wing started using the WW tail code, thus becoming a two-tail code wing, although only two GA tail coded F-4Gs were noted. The switch to F-4Gs was completed on July 12, 1980.

The 39th TFTS was also assigned on July 1, 1977, with both standard F-4Cs and Wild Weasel F-4Cs, and on May 11, 1984, was replaced by the 563rd TFS when conversion to the F-4G was complete. The 434th TFS redesignated to the 434th TFTS while flying the F-4D and F-4E, and on January 1, 1977, the 434th was inactivated.

The Wild Weasel operations of the 561st TFS, 562nd TFTS, and 563rd TFS remained at George AFB and were transferred to the 37th TFW on March 30, 1981, and the wing was redesignated the 35th Tactical Training Wing on July 1, 1984. The wing status returned to the 35th TFW designation on October 5, 1989, when F-4E/G Wild Weasel operations were returned from the 37th TFW. The 561st TFS and the 562nd TFTS returned to 35th TFW with WW codes.

In 1991, the wing was redesignated the 35th Fighter Wing. This designation was short-lived as George AFB was due for closure in 1993, and the 35th FW inactivated. All components having been inactivated or transferred, and the Weasel role was passed to Idaho ANG. The 1st GAFTS moved to Holloman AFB, New Mexico as part of the 49th Fighter Wing.

F-4E-31 MC 66-0294, ex-Thunderbird aircraft with 35th TFW multi-colored tail cap. Note the lack of the Lead Computing Optical Sight on the cockpit glare shield, and the fake nose gun fairing. Photographed on June 9, 1977, at George AFB. *Photo by Tom Brewer*

35th TFW

October 1, 1971, until March 30, 1981
Squadron Tail Codes July 15, 1971, until 1972

GA	4435th CCTS	Replaced by 431st TFTS January 1976
GB	4546th TFTS/TFRS/TTS	
GC	4452nd CCTS	
GD	434th TFS	

GA All

December 1972, until March 30, 1981

GA	434th TFS	
GA	20th TFTS	December 1, 1972
GA	21st TFTS	December 1, 1972
GA	431st TFTS	January 1976 – October 1978
GA	561st TFS	1973
GA	562nd TFTS	1974
GA	563rd TFS	1975
GA	39th TFTS/563rd TFS	July 1977

35th TFW/35th TTW

March 30, 1981, until 1993*

GA	434th TFS	
GA	20th TFTS	
GA	21st TFTS	
WW	561st TFS	Returned to the 35th on October 5, 1989
WW	562nd TFTS	Returned to the 35th on October 5, 1989
WW	563rd TFS	Returned to the 35th on October 5, 1989

* The 35th TFW was redesignated the 35th TTW on July 1, 1984. Both the 35th TFW with F-4Es, and the 37th TFW Wild Weasels (F-4Es and F-4Gs) were based at George from March 30, 1981 through October 5, 1989. On October 5, 1989, the 35th TFW absorbed the units of the 37th TFW.

35th TFW/35th TTW

F-4E-37 MC 68-0355, 35th flagship right side photographed at George AFB, in August 1973. The tail number has been modified to read 68-35 by painting over the second 5 in the 355 section of the tail number. *Photo by James P. Loomis*

F-4E-37 MC 68-0355, left side. The tail number has been modified to read 68-35 by painting over the second 5 in the tail number. Photographed at George AFB, on June 23, 1972. *Don Logan Collection*

F-4E-37 MC 33 68-0351, marked as the 35th TFW flagship, photographed on October 7, 1983. *Photo by Brian C. Rogers*

F-4E-33 MC 66-0357, marked as the 35th TTW flagship, photographed on February 16, 1988. *Photo by Jim Tunney*

F-4E-33 MC 66-0357, marked as the 35th TTW flagship, photographed in June 1989. *Photo by Mick Roth*

F-4E-33 MC 66-0372, marked as the 35th TTW flagship, photographed in March 1989. *Photo by Mick Roth*

F-4G-44 MC 69-7270, marked as the 35th TFW flagship in 561st TFS markings, photographed in November 1980. *Don Logan Collection*

F-4G-36 MC 68-0243, marked as the 35th TFW flagship in 562nd TFW Squadron markings, photographed in February 1981. *Photo by Jim Rotramel*

F-4G-44 MC 69-7574, marked as the 35th TFW flagship, photographed on December 1, 1990. *Don Logan Collection*

F-4G-43 MC 69-7263, marked as the 35th TFW flagship, photographed in May 1990. *Photo by Mick Roth*

4452nd CCTS

F-4D-31 MC 65-671 of the 4452nd CCTS, photographed on April 12, 1972, at McConnell AFB, Kansas. *Photo by Bill Malerba*

F-4D-29 MC 66-7489 of the 4452nd CCTS, on May 31, 1972, at McChord AFB, Washington. *Photo by Doug Remington*

F-4E-35 MC 68-0395 of the 4452nd CCTS, on November 10, 1972, at Eglin AFB, Florida. *Photo by Tom Brewer*

4435th CCTS

F-4C-21 MC 64-659 of the 4435th CCTS, on January 8, 1972, at McChord AFB, Washington. *Photo by Doug Remington*

F-4D-25 64-956 of the 4435th CCTS, on June 15, 1972, at McChord AFB, Washington, marked with the original 4435th squadron emblem on the intake. After the 4546th TTS inactivated, the 4435th adopted the "Little Devil" emblem of the 4546th. *Photo by Doug Remington*

F-4C-22 MC 64-726 of the 4435th CCTS, on September 18, 1974, at George AFB, California. *Photo by Tom Brewer*

F-4D-28 MC 65-743 of the 4435th CCTS, on September 18, 1974, at George AFB, California. *Photo by Tom Brewer*

434th TFS

F-4E-40 MC 68-0479 of the 434th TFS, at Kelly AFB, Texas, on April 21, 1972. *Photo by Norman E. Taylor*

F-4E-30 MC 68-0395 of the 434th TFS, at Wright-Patterson AFB, Ohio, on January 18, 1972. *Photo by Tom Brewer*

F-4E-41 MC 68-0505 of the 434th TFS, at Eglin AFB, Florida, in February 1972. *Photo by Tom Brewer*

F-4E-39 MC 68-0450 of the 434th TFS, at Andrews AFB, on July 7, 1973. *Photo by Jack D. Morris*

F-4C-23 MC 64-0806 of the 434th TFS, on September 18, 1974. *Photo by Tom Brewer*

F-4D-14 MC 63-7432 of the 4546th TFRS, at Eglin AFB, on March 18, 1972. *Photo by Tom Brewer*

F-4C-19 63-7555 of the 431 TFS, at George AFB, on November 7, 1976. *Photo by Tom Brewer*

F-4C-21 MC 21 64-0672 of the 4535th TFTS, on October 20, 1971, at Kelly AFB, Texas. *Photo by Norman E. Taylor*

F-4E-38 MC 68-400 of the 4535th TFTS, at George AFB, on June 23, 1972. *Tom Brewer Collection*

20th TFTS

F-4E-35 MC 67-0333 of the 20th TFTS at George AFB, on March 19, 1983. *Photo by Scott R. Wilson*

F-4E-63 MC 75-0631 of the 20th TFTS, April 16, 1983. *Photo by Scott R. Wilson*

F-4E-35 MC 67-0333 of the 20th TFTS, at Fairchild AFB, Washington, on May 19, 1985. *Photo by Doug Remington*

F-4E-35 MC 67-0288 of the 20th TFTS, at George AFB, in October 1989. *Photo by Mick Roth*

F-4E-34 MC 67-0235 marked as the 20th TFTS flagship, at George AFB, on November 8, 1986. *Photo by Craig Kaston*

F-4E-35 MC 67-0299 marked as the 20th TFTS flagship, at George AFB, in May 1990. *Photo by Mick Roth*

F-4E-41 MC 68-0531 marked as the 20th TFTS flagship, at George AFB, on April 10, 1992. *Photo by Scott Van Aken*

F-4E-34 MC 67-0270 of the 20th TFTS with two MiG kills, at George AFB, in March 1990. *Photo by Mick Roth*

F-4E-35 MC 67-0301 of the 20th TFTS with one MiG kill, in May 1990. *Photo by Mick Roth*

1st GAFTS

F-4F-52 MC 72-1119 of the 20th TFTS German Air Force Training Squadron (GAFTS), at George AFB, on October 29, 1973. *Photo by Don Logan*

F-4F-52 MC 72-1117 of the 20th TFTS GAFTS, at George AFB, on October 29, 1973. *Photo by Don Logan*

F-4E-63 MC 75-0635 of the 20th TFTS marked as the 1st GAFTS flagship, at George AFB, in January 1989. Note the pointed shape of the multi-colored tail stripe. *Photo by Paul Minert*

F-4E-63 MC 75-0635 of the 20th TFTS marked as the 1st GAFTS flagship at George AFB, in May 1990. Note the rectangular shape of the multi-colored tail stripe. *Photo by Mick Roth*

F-4E-63 MC 75-0629 of the 20th TFTS GAFTS, at George AFB, in July 1990. *Photo by Paul Minert*

21st TFTS

F-4E-39 MC 68-0428 of the 21st TFTS, at George AFB, on September 18, 1974. *Photo by Tom Brewer*

F-4E-35 MC 67-0327 of the 21st TFTS with one MiG kill, at George AFB, on September 18, 1974. *Photo by Tom Brewer*

F-4D-27 MC 65-0660 of the 21st TFTS, at George AFB, on September 18, 1974. *Photo by Tom Brewer*

F-4E-35 MC 67-0301 of the 21st TFTS, in March 1980. *Don Logan Collection*

F-4E-42 MC 69-0298 of the 21st TFTS, in March 1980. Note the extra 0 in the tail number. This is because there are two F-4Es in the 1969 year group; 69-0298 and 69-7298. *Photo by Ben Knowles*

F-4E-32 MC 66-0333 of the 21st TFTS, at George AFB, on May 26, 1980. An extra 6 was added to the tail number to make the number applied to the tail 666333. It was the same on the left side. *Photo by Don Logan*

Seen here is a lineup on the George AFB flight line of eight F-4Es of the 21st TFTS, with F-4E-36 MC 67-0344 on the near end. Photographed in January 1987. *Don Logan Collection*

F-4E-36 MC 66-0334 of the 21st TFTS, at George AFB, on June 20, 1987. *Photo by Don McGarry*

F-4E-32 MC 66-0330 of the 21st TFTS at Peterson AFB, Colorado, on May 8, 1987. *Photo by Robert Greby*

F-4E-31 MC 66-0295 of the 21st TFTS, at George AFB, on June 6, 1987. *Photo by Bob Leavitt*

F-4E-35 MC 67-0301 of the 21st TFTS with one MiG kill, at George AFB, on October 18, 1989. *Photo by Mick Roth*

F-4E-54 MC 72-1482 marked as the 21st TFTS flagship, at George AFB, in May 1990. *Photo by Mick Roth*

F-4E-61 MC 74-1060 of the 21st TFTS, at George AFB, in March 1990. *Photo by Mick Roth*

F-4E-58 MC 73-1176 of the 21st TFTS, at George AFB, in December 1990. *Photo by Mick Roth*

39th TFTS

F-4D-28 MC 65-0752 of the 39th TFTS, at George AFB, in August 1973. *Photo by James P. Loomis*

F-4C-29 MC 64-0686 of the 39th TFTS taxiing at George AFB, in December 1974. *Photo by Frank McSorley*

F-4E-36 MC 67-0396 marked as the 39th TFTS flagship, in November 1983. *Don Logan Collection*

F-4E-34 MC 67-0270 of the 39th TFTS with a double MiG kill, at George AFB, on March 6, 1983. *Photo By Scott R. Wilson*

F-4E-37 MC 68-0338 of the 39th TFTS with a single MiG kill, at George AFB, on March 6, 1983. *Photo By Scott R. Wilson*

F-4E-38 MC 68-0371 of the 39th TFTS, at Davis-Monthan AFB, in September 1983. *Don Logan Collection*

431st TFTS

F-4E-42 MC 64-0259 of the 431st TFTS, on July 22, 1978, at George AFB. Note the small devil's head in the red fin cap and the reversed tail number presentation. *Photo by Don Logan*

F-4E-42 MC 69-0265 of the 431st TFTS, at George AFB, on July 24, 1979. *Photo by Phil Huston*

561st TFS

F-4E-49 MC 69-0265 of the 561st TFS taxiing at George AFB, in December 1974. *Photo by Frank McSorley*

F-4E-49 MC 66-0298 of the 561st TFS, at Holloman AFB, on December 7, 1979. *Photo by Bob Leavitt*

F-4E-63 MC 74-0663 of the 561st TFS, at George AFB, in March 1992. *Photo by Paul Minert*

F-4E-58 MC 73-0173 of the 561st TFS, at George AFB, in April 1992. *Photo by Scott Van Aken*

562nd TFTS

F-4E-38 MC 68-0390 of the 562nd TFTS, at Nellis AFB, on May 9, 1975. *Photo by Don Logan*

F-4E-33 MC 67-0329 ex-Thunderbird aircraft of the 562nd TFTS. Note the lack of the Lead Computing Optical Sight on the cockpit glare shield, the added extra communications antenna on the aircraft spine, and the fake nose gun fairing. Photographed on September 18, 1975. *Photo by Don Logan*

F-4E-63 MC 75-0629 of the 562nd TFTS, at George AFB, on June 9, 1977. *Photo by Tom Brewer*

F-4E-58 MC 73-1176 of the 562nd TFTS, at George AFB, on June 6, 1991. *Photo by David F. Brown*

563rd TFS

F-4C-22 MC 64-0726 of the 563rd TFS, in August 1973. *Photo by James P. Loomis*

F-4E-42 MC 69-0267 of the 563rd TFS, painted with a bad batch of tan paint, July 22, 1973. *Photo by Don Logan*

F-4E-42 MC 69-0237 of the 563rd TFS, on July 23, 1979. *Don Logan Collection*

F-4E-42 MC 69-0248 of the 563rd TFS, painted with a bad batch of tan paint photographed at George AFB, on July 22, 1973. *Photo by Don Logan*

35th TTW F-4Es
561st TFS

F-4E-62 MC 74-1650 of the 561st TFS, at Nellis AFB, in January 1989. *Don Logan Collection*

F-4E-60 MC 74-1045 of the 561st TFS, at George AFB, in December 1991. *Don Logan Collection*

562nd TFTS

F-4E-54 MC 72-1477 of the 562nd TFTS, at McConnell AFB, on April 1, 1990. *Photo by Don Logan*

F-4E-58 MC 73-1176 of the 562nd TFTS, at George AFB, on March 28, 1992. *Photo by Peter Wilson*

F-4E-58 MC 73-1183 of the 562nd TFTS, at George AFB, in May 1992. *Photo by Paul Minert*

F-4E-60 MC 74-1044 of the 562nd TFTS at George AFB, on March 28, 1992. *Photo by Peter Wilson*

F-4E-60 MC 74-1045 of the 562nd TFTS, at George AFB, in June 1991. *Photo by David F. Brown*

F-4E-62 MC 74-1653 of the 562nd TFTS, at George AFB, in October 1989. *Photo by Mick Roth*

35th TTW F-4Gs
39th TFTS

F-4G-43 MC 69-7208 of the 39th TFTS marked as "City of Victorville Sweet Sixteen," on September 22, 1978, taxiing at George AFB. *Photo by Tom Brewer*

caption F-4G-43 MC 69-7235 of the 39th TFTS, at George AFB, on May 24, 1980. *Photo by Don Logan*

F-4G-43 MC 69-7257 of the 39th TFTS, at Nellis AFB, in November 1980. *Keith Svendsen*

F-4G-44 MC 69-7289 of the 39th TFTS, Nellis AFB, on June 20, 1980. *Don Logan Collection*

F-4C-24 MC 64-0847 of the 39th TFTS, at George AFB, on July 22, 1978. The small red WW in the white tail stripe indicates this is a F-4C Wild Weasel. *Photo by Don Logan*

561st TFS

F-4G-42 MC 69-0241 of the 561st TFS, at Nellis, on December 8, 1980. *Don Logan Collection*

F-4G-42 MC 69-0271 of the 561st TFS, at Nellis, on December 8, 1980. *Don Logan Collection*

F-4G-42 MC 69-0293 of the 561st TFS, at George AFB, in October 1989. *Photo by Mick Roth*

F-4G-44 MC 69-7561 in 561st TFS, fiftieth anniversary markings, at George AFB, in May 1992. *Photo by Paul Minert*

F-4G-44 MC 69-7561 in 561st TFS, fiftieth anniversary markings, at George AFB, in May 1992. *Photo by Paul Minert*

F-4G-44 MC 69-7561 of the 561st TFS flagship, on October 11, 1991. *Photo by Keith Snyder*

F-4G-43 MC 69-7260 of the 561st TFS, at George AFB, on June 7, 1991. *Photo by David F. Brown*

562nd TFTS

F-4G-42 MC 69-0292 of the 562nd TFTS flagship, at George AFB, in March 1987. *Don Logan Collection*

F-4G-43 MC 69-7251 of the 562nd TFTS, at Luke AFB, on June 4, 1991. *Photo by Kevin Patrick*

F-4G-44 MC 69-7289 of the 562nd TFTS, at George AFB, in May 1992. *Photo by Paul Minert*

F-4G-44 MC 69-7298 of the 562nd TFTS, at George AFB, in December 1991. *Don Logan Collection*

F-4C-20 MC 63-7656 of the 562nd TFTS, at George AFB, on November 7, 1976. The small red WW in the white tail stripe indicates this is a F-4C Wild Weasel. *Photo by Bill Malerba*

F-4C-20 MC 63-7564 of the 562nd TFTS, at George AFB, on July 17, 1977. The small red WW in the white tail stripe indicates this is a F-4C Wild Weasel. *Photo by Bill Malerba*

563rd TFS

F-4C-18 MC 63-0481 of the 563rd TFS, on November 7, 1977, at George AFB. The small red WW in the white tail stripe indicates this is a F-4C Wild Weasel. *Photo by Tom Brewer*

F-4C-24 MC 564-0847 of the 563rd TFS, on November 7, 1977, at George AFB. The small red WW in the white tail stripe indicates this is a F-4C Wild Weasel. *Photo by Tom Brewer*

F-4G-43 MC 69-0304 of the 563rd TFS, at George AFB, on June 25, 1979. *Don Logan Collection*

F-4G-43 MC 69-7207 of the 563rd TFS, at George AFB, in October 1979. *Don Logan Collection*

F-4G-45 MC 69-7582 of the 563rd TFS, at George AFB, in October 1979. *Photo by Norman E. Taylor*

F-4G-45 MC 69-7584 of the 563rd TFS, at George AFB. *Don Logan Collection*

37TH TACTICAL FIGHTER WING

The 37th Tactical Fighter Wing was activated at Phu Cat AB, Republic of South Vietnam (RSVN), on March 1, 1967, as an F-100 Super Sabre wing. On June 15, 1969, two F-4D units, the 389th TFS and 480th TFS, were transferred from the 366th TFW at Da Nang AB, RSVN. The 37th TFW inactivated on March 31, 1970, and was replaced by the 12th TFW.

The 37th TFW was reactivated on March 30, 1981, at George AFB, California, taking control of the Wild Weasel assets from the co-based 35th TFW. The F-4Es and F-4Gs of the 561st TFS, 562nd TFTS, and the 563rd TFS were tail coded WW. On October 5, 1989, the 37th TFW moved to Tonopah as the first F-117 Nighthawk wing. On the same day, the Wild Weasel assets returned to the 35th TFW and the 563rd TFS inactivated.

Both the 35th TFW with F-4Es and the 37th TFW Wild Weasels (F-4Es and F-4Gs) were based at George from March 30, 1981 through October 5, 1989. On October 5, 1989, the 35th TFW absorbed the units of the 37th TFW.

37th TFW
March 30, 1981, until October 5, 1989

WW	561st TFS	F-4E & F-4G
WW	562nd TFTS	F-4E & F-4G
WW	563rd TFS	F-4E & F-4G

37th TFW

F-4G-42 MC 69-0237 of the 563rd TFS marked as the 37th TFW flagship, on August 3, 1984. *Photo by Brian C. Rogers*

F-4G-42 MC 69-0251 marked as the 37th TFW flagship with all three TFS patches on the intake, photographed at Luke AFB, on February 21, 1987. *Photo by Bob Leavitt*

37th TFW F-4Es
561st TFS

F-4E-32 MC 66-0301 of the 561st TFS, on April 24, 1983. *Don Logan Collection*

F-4E-38 MC 66-0370 of the 561st TFS, photographed on May 25, 1987. *Photo by Robert Greby*

F-4E-35 MC 67-0328 of the 561st TFS, photographed on April 11, 1986. *Photo by Rick Morgan*

F-4E-42 MC 69-0261 of the 561st TFS, photographed on March 2, 1985. *Don Logan Collection*

F-4E-54 MC 74-1060 of the 561st TFS, photographed on February 24, 1989. *Photo by Mike Anselmo*

F-4E-63 MC 74-1642 of the 561st TFS, photographed on September 14, 1989. *Don Logan Collection*

562nd TFTS

F-4E-34 MC 69-0280 of the 562nd TFS, at George AFB, photographed on August 30, 1984. *Photo by Brian C. Rogers*

F-4E-32 MC 66-0298 of the 562nd TFS, at George AFB, photographed on March 13, 1987. *Photo by Phil Huston*

F-4E-60 MC 74-0662 of the 562nd TFS, at George AFB, photographed in January 1989. *Don Logan Collection*

F-4E-33 MC 66-0356 of the 562nd TFS, photographed on May 4, 1985. *Don Logan Collection*

563rd TFS

F-4E-60 MC 74-1048 of the 563rd TFS at George AFB, photographed on June 6, 1987. *Photo Bob Leavitt*

F-4E-47 MC 69-0298 of the 563rd TFS, at George AFB, photographed in August 1986. *Photo Jim Goodall*

F-4E-54 MC 72-1485 of the 563rd TFS, at George AFB, photographed on September 23, 1989. *Photo by Phil Huston*

F-4E-61 MC 74-1628 of the 563rd TFS, at George AFB, photographed on February 24, 1989. *Photo by Mike Anselmo*

37th TFW F-4Gs
561st TFS

F-4G-44 MC 69-7301 of the 561st TFS, photographed in May 1981. *Don Logan Collection*

F-4G-42 MC 69-0293 marked as the 561st TFS flagship, photographed in June 1983. *Don Logan Collection*

F-4G-44 MC 69-7561 marked as the 561st TFS flagship, photographed in March 1987. *Don Logan Collection*

F-4G-44 MC 69-7561 marked as the 561st TFS flagship, at Peterson AFB, Colorado, photographed in May 1987. *Photo by Robert Greby*

McDonnell Douglas F-4 Phantom II at George Air Force Base, California 1964-1992

F-4G-42 MC 69-0297 marked as the 561st TFS, at George AFB, photographed on March 13, 1987. *Photo by Phil Huston*

F-4G-44 MC 69-7561 marked as the 561st TFS flagship, photographed on February 24, 1989. *Photo by Mike Anselmo*

F-4G-42 MC 69-0251 of the 561st TFS, photographed on May 9, 1988. *Photo by Ray Leader*

F-4G-45 MC 69-7581 of the 561st TFS, photographed on February 24, 1989. *Photo by Mike Anselmo*

562nd TFTS

F-4G-42 MC 69-0277 of the 562nd TFTS, photographed in June 1982. *Don Logan Collection*

F-4G-43 MC 69-7235 of the 562nd TFTS, at George AFB, photographed in December 1982. *Photo By Scott R. Wilson*

F-4G-44 MC 69-7288 marked as the 562nd TFS, flagship at Peterson AFB, on May 8, 1987. *Photo by Robert Greby*

F-4G-44 MC 69-7288 marked as the 562nd TFS, flagship June 1987. *Photo by Norman E. Taylor*

McDonnell Douglas F-4 Phantom II at George Air Force Base, California 1964-1992

F-4G-42 MC 69-0272 of the 562nd TFS, on August 30, 1984. *Photo by Brian C. Rogers*

F-4G-42 MC 69-0254 of the 562nd TFS, at George AFB, on March 28, 1992. *Photo by Peter Wilson*

563rd TFS

F-4G-45 MC 69-7587 of the 563rd TFS, on November 8, 1981. *Don Logan Collection*

F-4G-44 MC 69-7574 of the 563rd TFS, at George AFB, in September 1981. *Don Logan Collection*

F-4G-42 MC 69-0252 of the 563rd TFS, at George AFB, in April 1981. *Don Logan Collection*

F-4G-42 MC 69-0261 of the 563rd TFS, at George AFB, in May 1983. *Don Logan Collection*

F-4G-42 MC 69-7237 of the 563rd TFS, on February 23, 1982. *Photo by Norman E. Taylor*

F-4G-45 MC 69-7581 of the 563rd TFS, on October 27, 1962. *Don Logan Collection*

F-4G-42 MC 69-0281 marked as the 563rd TFS flagship, March 9, 1987. *Photo by Jim Wooley*

F-4G-43 MC 69-7232 of the 563rd TFS, at George AFB, on February 1, 1984. *Photo by Keith Svendsen*

F-4G-43 MC 69-7204 marked as the 563rd TFS flagship, at George AFB, in September 1989. *Don Logan Collection*

F-4G-43 MC 69-0304 of the 563rd TFS, at George AFB, on February 16, 1988. *Photo by Jim Tunney*

F-4 UNITS GEORGE AFB, CALIFORNIA: TAIL CODE/UNITS TABLE

479th TFW
1965, until October 1, 1971

GA	68th TFS	December 6, 1965 to 4535th CCTS
GB	431st TFS	early 1965 to 4546th TFTS/TFRS
GC	434th TFS	December 6, 1965 to 4452nd CCTS
GD	476th TFS	early 1965 to 434th TFS
GE	4452nd CCTS	January 16, 1968 to UH-1s

35th TFW
October 1, 1971, until March 30, 1981
Squadron Tail Codes July 15, 1971, until 1972

GA	4435th CCTS replaced by 431st TFTS January 1976
GB	4546th TFTS/TFRS/TTS
GC	4452nd CCTS
GD	434th TFS

GA All –
December 1972, until March 30, 1981

GA	434th TFS	
GA	20th TFTS	December 1, 1972
GA	21st TFTS	December 1, 1972
GA	431st TFTS	January 1, 1976 – October 1978
GA	561st TFS	1973
GA	562nd TFTS	1974
GA	563rd TFS	1975
GA	39th TFTS/563rd TFS	July 1977

35th TFW
March 30, 1981, until October 5, 1989*

GA	434th TFS
GA	20th TFTS
GA	21st TFTS

37th TFW
March 30, 1981, until October 5, 1989*

WW	561st TFS
WW	562nd TFTS
WW	563rd TFS

35th TFW
October 5, 1989, until 1993*

GA	1st GAFTS
GA	20th TFTS
GA	21st TFTS
WW	561st TFS
WW	562nd TFTS
WW	563rd TFS

* Both the 35th TFW with F-4Es and the 37th TFW Wild Weasels (F-4Es and F-4Gs) were based at George from March 30, 1981, through October 5, 1989. On October 5, 1989, the 35th TFW absorbed the units of the 37th TFW.

APPENDICES

BLOCK NUMBERS

U.S. AIR FORCE F-4C-15-MC
A.F. SERIAL 63-7407

F-4C-15-MC
A.F. SERIAL 62-12199 and
A.F. SERIAL 63-7407 thru 63-7420

F-4C-16-MC
A.F. SERIAL 63-7421 thru 63-7442

F-4C-17-MC
A.F. SERIAL 63-7443 thru 63-7468

F-4C-18-MC
A.F. SERIAL 63-7469 thru 63-7526

F-4C-19-MC
A.F. SERIAL 63-7527 thru 63-7597

F-4C-20-MC
A.F. SERIAL 63-7598 thru 63-7662

F-4C-21-MC
A.F. SERIAL 63-7663 thru 63-7713
and 64-654 thru 64-672

F-4C-22-MC
A.F. SERIAL 64-673 thru 64-737

F-4C-23-MC
A.F. SERIAL 64-738 thru 64-817

F-4C-24-MC
A.F. SERIAL 64-818 thru 64-881

F-4C-25-MC
A.F. SERIAL 64-882 thru 64-928

F-4D-24-MC
A.F. SERIAL 64-929 thru 64-937

F-4D-25-MC
A.F. SERIAL 64-938 thru 64-963

F-4D-26-MC
A.F. SERIAL 64-964 thru 64-980
and 65-580 thru 65-611

F-4D-27-MC
A.F. SERIAL 65-612 thru 65-665

F-4D-28-MC
A.F. SERIAL 65-666 thru 65-770

F-4D-29-MC
A.F. SERIAL 65-771 thru 65-801 and
66-226 thru 66-283 and
66-7455 thru 66-7504

F-4D-30-MC
A.F. SERIAL 66-7505 thru 66-7650

F-4D-31-MC
A.F. SERIAL 66-7651 thru 66-7774
and 66-8685 thru 66-8698

F-4D-32-MC
A.F. SERIAL 66-8699 thru 66-8786

F-4D-33-MC
A.F. SERIAL 66-8787 thru 66-8825

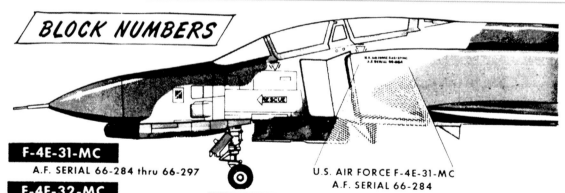

BLOCK NUMBERS

U.S. AIR FORCE F-4E-31-MC
A.F. SERIAL 66-284

F-4E-31-MC
A.F. SERIAL 66-284 thru 66-297

F-4E-32-MC
A.F. SERIAL 66-298 thru 66-338

F-4E-33-MC
A.F. SERIAL 66-339 thru 66-382
A.F. SERIAL 67-208 thru 67-219

F-4E-34-MC
A.F. SERIAL 67-220 thru 67-282

F-4E-35-MC
A.F. SERIAL 67-283 thru 67-341

F-4E-36-MC
A.F. SERIAL 67-342 thru 67-398

F-4E-37-MC
A.F. SERIAL 68-303 thru 68-365

F-4E-38-MC
A.F. SERIAL 68-366 thru 68-395
A.F. SERIAL 68-400 thru 68-409

F-4E-39-MC
A.F. SERIAL 68-410 thru 68-413
A.F. SERIAL 68-418 thru 68-433
A.F. SERIAL 68-438 thru 68-451

F-4E-40-MC
A.F. SERIAL 68-452 thru 68-453
A.F. SERIAL 68-458 thru 68-468
A.F. SERIAL 68-473 thru 68-483
A.F. SERIAL 68-488 thru 68-494

F-4E-41-MC
A.F. SERIAL 68-495 thru 68-498
A.F. SERIAL 68-503 thru 68-518
A.F. SERIAL 68-526 thru 68-538

F-4E-42-MC
A.F. SERIAL 69-236 thru 69-303

F-4E-43-MC
A.F. SERIAL 69-304 thru 69-307
A.F. SERIAL 69-7201 thru 69-7260

F-4E-44-MC
A.F. SERIAL 69-7261 thru 69-7303
A.F. SERIAL 69-7546 thru 69-7578

F-4E-45-MC
A.F. SERIAL 69-7579 thru 69-7589

F-4E-48-MC
A.F. SERIAL 71-224 thru 71-247

F-4E-49-MC
A.F. SERIAL 71-1070 thru 71-1093

F-4E-50-MC
A.F. SERIAL 71-1391 thru 71-1402
A.F. SERIAL 72-121 thru 72-138

F-4E-51-MC
A.F. SERIAL 72-139 thru 72-144
A.F. SERIAL 72-157 thru 72-159

F-4E-52-MC
A.F. SERIAL 72-160 thru 72-165

F-4E-53-MC
A.F. SERIAL 72-166 thru 72-168
A.F. SERIAL 72-1407

F-4E-54-MC
A.F. SERIAL 72-1476 thru 72-1489

F-4E-55-MC
A.F. SERIAL 72-1490 thru 72-1497

F-4E-56-MC
A.F. SERIAL 72-1498 thru 72-1499

F-4E-57-MC
A.F. SERIAL 73-01157 thru 73-01164

F-4E-58-MC
A.F SERIAL 73-01165 thru 73-01184

F-4E-59-MC
A.F. SERIAL 73-01185 thru 73-01204

F-4E-60-MC
A.F. SERIAL 74-00643 thru 74-00666
A.F. SERIAL 74-01038 thru 74-01049

F-4E-61-MC
A.F. SERIAL 74-01050 thru 74-01061
A.F. SERIAL 74-01620 thru 74-01637

F-4E-62-MC
A.F. SERIAL 74-01638 thru 74-01653

F-4E-63-MC
A.F. SERIAL 75-00628 thru 75-00637

BLOCK NUMBERS

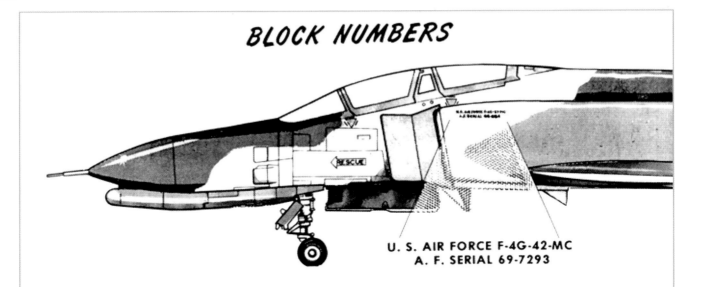

U. S. AIR FORCE F-4G-42-MC
A. F. SERIAL 69-7293

F-4G-42-MC

A.F. SERIAL 69-0236 thru 69-0255
A.F. SERIAL 69-0258 thru 69-0261
A.F. SERIAL 69-0263 thru 69-0265
A.F. SERIAL 69-0267
A.F. SERIAL 69-0269 thru 69-0275
A.F. SERIAL 69-0277 thru 69-0281
A.F. SERIAL 69-0284 thru 69-0286
A.F. SERIAL 69-0290 thru 69-0293
A.F. SERIAL 69-0297

F-4G-43-MC

A.F. SERIAL 69-0303 thru 69-0307
A.F. SERIAL 69-7201 thru 69-7202
A.F. SERIAL 69-7204
A.F. SERIAL 69-7206 thru 69-7212
A.F. SERIAL 69-7214 thru 69-7220
A.F. SERIAL 69-7223
A.F. SERIAL 69-7228
A.F. SERIAL 69-7231 thru 69-7236
A.F. SERIAL 69-7251 thru 69-7254
A.F. SERIAL 69-7256 thru 69-7258
A.F. SERIAL 69-7260

F-4G-44-MC

A.F. SERIAL 69-7261 thru 69-7263
A.F. SERIAL 69-7267
A.F. SERIAL 69-7270
A.F. SERIAL 69-7272
A.F. SERIAL 69-7286 thru 69-7291
A.F. SERIAL 69-7293 thru 69-7295
A.F. SERIAL 69-7297 thru 69-7298
A.F. SERIAL 69-7300 thru 69-7303
A.F. SERIAL 69-7546
A.F. SERIAL 69-7550 thru 69-7551
A.F. SERIAL 69-7556 thru 69-7558
A.F. SERIAL 69-7560 thru 69-7561
A.F. SERIAL 69-7566
A.F. SERIAL 69-7571 thru 69-7572
A.F. SERIAL 69-7574

F-4G-45-MC

A.F. SERIAL 69-7579 thru 69-7583
A.F. SERIAL 69-7586 thru 69-7588

	F-4C	F-4D	F-4E	F-4E AFTER TO 1F-4E-626	F-4G
ENGINES	J79−GE−15	J79−GE− 15/15A/15E	J79−GE− 17A/E/F/G	J79−GE− 17A/E/F/G	J79−GE− 17A/C/E/F/G
NO. 7 FUEL CELL	NO	NO	YES	YES	YES
RAM AIR TURBINE	YES	YES	NO	NO	NO
HYDRAULIC WING FOLD	YES	YES	NO	NO	NO
INTERNALLY MOUNTED GUN	NO	NO	YES	YES	NO
RADAR SET	AN/APQ−100	AN/APQ−109	AN/APQ−120	AN/APQ−120 MODIFIED	AN/APQ−120 MODIFIED
INTERCEPT COMPUTER	AN/APA−157	AN/APA−157 or AN/APA−165	AN/APQ−120	AN/APQ−120	AN/APQ−120
OPTICAL SIGHT	FIXED	AN/ASG−22	AN/ASG−26	AN/ASG−26 MODIFIED	AN/APQ−30 MODIFIED
TISEO (AN/ASX−1)	NO	NO	71−237 AND UP	AN/ASX−1 MODIFIED	NO
RADAR RECEIVING SET	NO	NO	NO	NO	AN/APR−47
WEAPONS RELEASE COMPUTER	NONE	AN/ASQ−91	AN/ASQ−91	NO	NO
INERTIAL NAVIGATION SET	AN/ASN−48	AN/ASN−63	AN/ASN−63	NO	NO
NAVIGATION COMPUTER	AN/ASN−46	AN/ASN−46A	AN/ASN−46A	NO	NO
AUXILIARY POWER UNIT	NO	NO	68−452 AND UP	YES	YES
SELF SEALING FUSELAGE FUEL CELLS	NO	NO	68−495 AND UP	YES	YES
LEADING EDGE BOUNDARY LAYER CONTROL	YES	YES	NO	NO	NO
LEADING EDGE SLATS	NO	NO	YES	YES	YES
ATTITUDE REFERENCE BOMBING COMPUTER SET	AN/AJB−7	AN/AJB−7	AN/AJB−7	AN/AJB−7 MODIFIED	AN/AJB−7 MODIFIED
DIGITAL MODULAR AVIONICS SYSTEM (DMAS)	NO	NO	NO	YES	YES
AUTOMATIC FLIGHT CONTROL SYSTEM (AFCS)	AN/ASA−32J	AN/ASA−32J	AN/ASA−32J	AN/ASA−32J MODIFIED	AN/ASA−32J MODIFIED

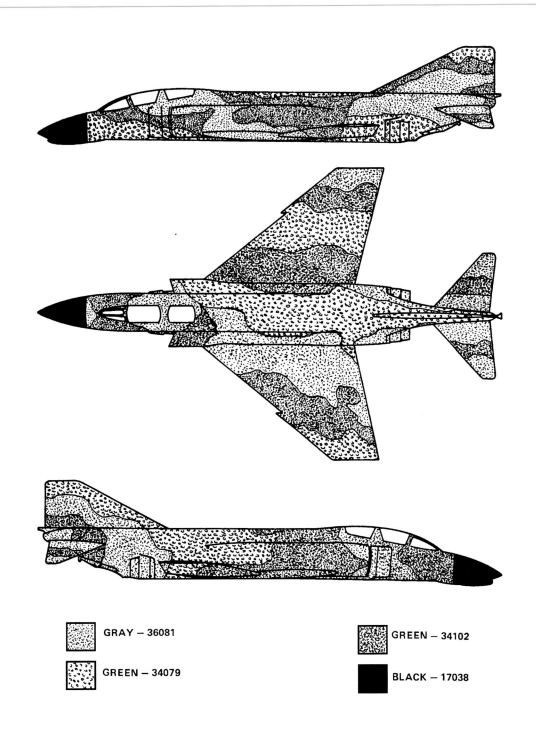

GRAY — 36081

GREEN — 34102

GREEN — 34079

BLACK — 17038

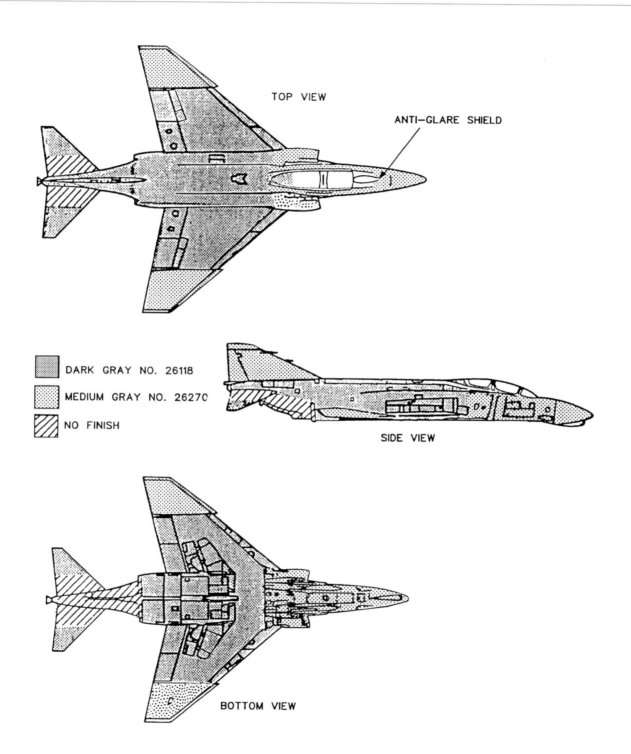

TOP VIEW

ANTI-GLARE SHIELD

DARK GRAY NO. 26118

MEDIUM GRAY NO. 26270

NO FINISH

SIDE VIEW

BOTTOM VIEW

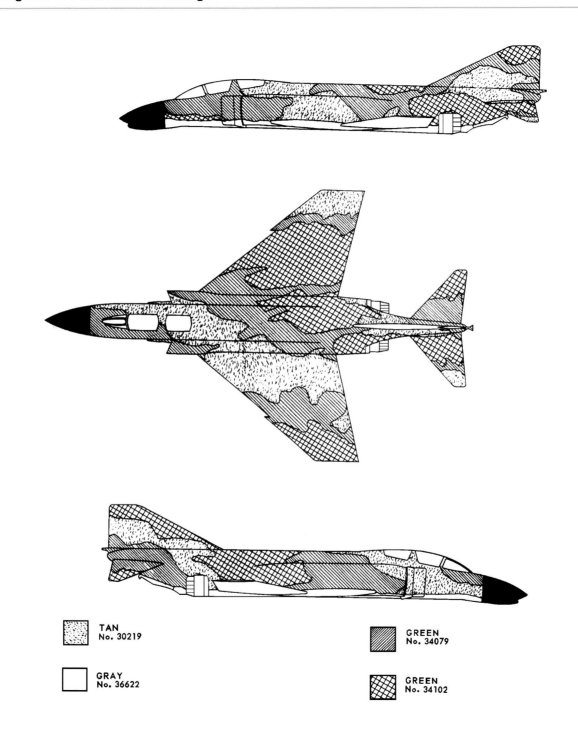

TAN
No. 30219

GRAY
No. 36622

GREEN
No. 34079

GREEN
No. 34102